NORMAL
BRITISH
CHRISTMAS?

The different and daft ways we celebrate the season

Jack !

compiled by TEE DOBINSON

Enjoy ! Tee Dobinson x

Published by BAIZDON

19 Half Moon Lane
London SE24 9JU
www.baizdon.com

Designed by Johnny Morris

A CIP catalogue record for this book is available from the British Library.
Printed in Great Britain

ISBN 978-0-9574012-7-3
eISBN 978-0-9574012-5-9

Contents

Contents

THE NORMAL BRITISH CHRISTMAS?

INTRODUCTION

Eleven layers are ten too many...

So what is the *Normal British Christmas?* To find out I interviewed people across Britain and discovered a huge range of amazing, poignant and possibly slightly crazy traditions, that all seem perfectly normal to the families that enjoy them. No one thought that how they celebrate is unique, it is just what happens (and usually what has always happened). While people would say *'we just do the normal'* or *'the same as everyone else'* it soon became clear that the pattern of each family's Christmas was as individual as a snowflake, with everyone knowing the intricate details and the exact order of events that makes up the *Normal British Christmas* for them. This does makes it very easy to get Christmas wrong when you spend it with someone else, and this happening to me was really where the book began.

I was looking forward to my first Christmas with my future husband's family. I had wrapped each of the children's presents with eleven layers of wrapping paper and popped a gold chocolate coin in between each layer. It will be such fun I thought, imagining shouts of joy as layers of paper fly across the room and gold chocolate coins roll around. The children would be happy, the adults (maybe even my future mother-in-law) all delighted and I will have joined seamlessly into another family's Christmas. It didn't work out quite like that.

Christmas Day arrived and strangely the Morris family didn't open their presents straightaway. No, they waited until the afternoon. Definitely not normal. Then, rather than the Dobinson all-at-once mania of present opening they had a one-at-a-time ceremony, with everyone watching each person open each gift in turn. Picture the scene, eleven layers of wrapping paper, multiplied by four children, multiplied by two presents each, equals 88 gold coins. The novelty wore off fairly quickly.

Had my future husband been from another country or culture I would have expected differences, researched and prepared for them even. I just didn't dream someone who lived down the road would celebrate Christmas so differently from me. Now I know better. I hope you enjoy reading about the *Normal British Christmas*. Prepare to be amazed. **TD**

TRADITIONS

It's a selection box!

TRADITIONS

To get people thinking about their
Normal British Christmas traditions, I asked
them what were the things that Christmas
wouldn't feel right without. In our house for
instance, I said, we have a *Peter Rabbit* holly
dish that I bought when I was pregnant.
It has to be used at every December
meal leading up to and including
Christmas Day.

TRADITIONS

"Mamma used to play Christmas Carols from the 13th December till the 6th of January. Every day!" MICAELA.S

"The Trifle Pea. Whoever gets the pea hidden in the trifle gets to open their presents first" BRYONY.Y

"On Christmas Eve we would always write out our Christmas wish list, light it and send it up the chimney. Thinking about that now it was way too late for our parents to do anything about it!" SARA.F

"The ritual of choosing the trees, invariably taking one back and swapping when my wife decides it isn't 'tree-like enough'. Thank goodness we live in the countryside and have a choice of understanding farms!" MARTIN.K

"I buy a new version of *The Night Before Christmas* every year by Clement C Moore and write a summary of our year in the front of it. We have 15 so far." DEBRA.W

"I always bake a Christmas cake and mince pies and make my own rollmops." RUTH.P

"I have a collection of Christmas hats, built up over the years – sparkly, elves ears, Santa and even a turkey. We all wear one for one course and then swop. The turkey hat looks really good on the guys with no hair." DIANE.E.G

"My fiancé's family have a tradition of writing a short poem to each receiver. Sometimes they rhyme but it's not required. It is usually a cryptic poem about the gift to make you try and guess what it is (usually it is impossible!)" AMY.H

"I do not know when this started (many years ago) but every time we open a selection box we shout at the top of our voices IT'S A SELECTION BOX! We buy these on purpose just to do it and for some reason then take a cheesy photo!" SALLY-ANNE.E

"No Christmas Tree but always a Christmas Vase, I put decorations all around the base." GILLIAN.B

"I'm always dressed, my sister's in her pyjamas." RICH S

"Graham trying to get us to have a small tree (and failing) and have six silver balls only on it (ditto)." NANCY.W

"We have a little wooden golden bell that has been handed down over the generations. It's always taken outside and rung by Tinkerbell to announce Father Christmas`s arrival, a sign to close eyes tight and pretend to be asleep. Last year the younger generation were all away skiing, so my daughter rang the bell from her mobile to France and Austria. They could hear it really well." JUNE.B

"Phil played Frisbee at Uni and, as he's always trying to get us to play, someone always gets a Frisbee as a present. We have quite a collection. Nobody ever plays but they're very handy as plant holders." CAROLYN.W

"My wife makes a very special trifle on Christmas Eve – one spoonful would put you very much over the driving limit! And I remembered something else, she has to be allowed to watch *Love Actually* a few days before Christmas arrives!" MARTIN.K

"I always go to Harrods with my Mum on the Friday before Christmas – we always buy Truffle Cheese, it's really delicious." LOTTIE.M

"Before Christmas my Dad would write 'Merry Christmas and Happy New Year' on all the mirrors in our house in felt tip pen which I always liked." JOHNNY.M

"The Christmas ornaments come out, also the Christmas candles, crockery, tea-towels, hand towels, hand soap and lotion." JILL.S

"I have a Christmas book where I've written down every present I've ever given them. I started it in 1987." JUDITH.Y

"My little brother, now 23, still wakes me up at 5am and yells, it's Christmas!" NAJIA.K

"Our dog Flossie can eat chocolates from tree including the foil, she leaves the string and the tree intact." SALLY.W

"Bob has to fully investigate and analyse every present, who it's from, what does it do, where was it made. The process can take more than 10 minutes per present."
SUE.M

"We always held hands and, as *I'm Dreaming of a White Christmas* started playing, went into the front room together." JANE.B

"We all sit on the sofa and Mum brings the presents in and we have to act surprised." HAYLEY.S

"We have The Christmas Quiz which my brother brings with him (my Mum and my Gran always team up) – we do this during pudding. We always flame the pudding."
EMMA.R

"One year my Grandad called our snowman a Winter Person, it didn't catch on." BRETT.C

"We always have Table Presents – a small wrapped present with your place setting and you open it before lunch. They're not from anyone (although always bought by me)." FRANCES.S

9

"Christmas is all about baking in our house. The house is always filled with cake! We also have a set of six jewel-coloured mini tumblers which are the only thing that mulled wine will be drunk from. They come out every year." NATASHA.W

"I always put a torch in the Stockings." MAUREEN.B

"We start with Bucks Fizz for breakfast. Move onto the pub up the road for drinks which include tequila and Sambuca shots at noon, and then stroll home for lunch, which Mum usually has in the oven before we hit the pub, as she's usually a bit tiddly by the time we get back!" CHARLOTTE.H

"My daughter Tia always makes take-home jars, adorned with ribbon and bows, of peanut brittle, Christmas bark & mint chocolates as presents for family members." MICHELLE.T

"Different sack for everyone – added to collection as they are born or join the family, some with names on that are 35 and 37 years old." DIANE.G

"I iced the cake every year making a peaky snow surface and adding the family traditional decorations – a tiny postbox, a gold Father Christmas, a piece of plastic holly and Bambi. One year the family were presented with smooth snow (I had discovered roll-out fondant icing). "What has happened to the cake" everyone cried, despite the tiny postbox, the gold Father Christmas, the piece of plastic holly and Bambi all being present. "It's the snow, it's not right" they said. The cake went back to the kitchen, the fondant icing came off (and went into the bin) and I made the peaky snow." TINA.K

"The whole season is chocolate chocolate chocolate"
DEBRA.W

"I have a Tupperware dish that is split into sections for all the nibbles. It was my Mum's and was always my job as the oldest to fill it up for Christmas. I got it when they went to Cyprus and my daughter had the job of filling it this year." LAURA.B

FIRST POST
The tradition of commercial Christmas cards was started by Sir Henry Cole in London in 1843. He commissioned a card featuring a family drinking wine. One sold for £8,469 in 2010.

"Dad always used to carve now it's me!" DIANE.E.G

"St John's has a Live Nativity with animals and a procession around the village. Every year Jan, the publican of *The British Oak*, comes out and says there is no room at the inn." ANDREW.B

"Francesca is adamant that we must have crackers. I usually make them because I don't like the way manufacturers put the contents on the back of the box. Where is the surprise in that?!" CATHERINE.M.S

"I always make the puddings using my Grandmother's recipe. We do this on the Sunday before the start of Advent. Everyone gets to stir the pudding and make a wish (Stir-it-up Sunday.)" ANNE.P

"On Christmas Day at noon we lift our glasses and toast our friends and family wherever they are - all over the world – and they all do it at the same time too." JOY.B

"We always go to Waitrose for the Christmas food shopping – it's the only time we go there." SAMANTHA.D

"I have a favourite candle holder that is a winter scene and when the tea light is lit it is a winter village all lit up – very pretty. Once this comes out it is kept lit all the time we are home." CHILLY.H

"Our friends always have a tree decorating party. We all go and everyone adds something to the tree." SIMON.P

"I always add a rocking-horse gift tag my Dad gave me when I was 18 to a mini-Christmas tree in my bedroom." FRANCES.S

"We have a Christmas bell that we all like which has to sit in the same special place each year." CHARLOTTE.K

"My daughter and I sang carols at the local church crib service and saw the nativity scene. A lovely tradition that I will carry on every year." TINA.T

"Every year my Grandma says she's given all the present money to charity – every year." TIM.P

"The cat (via Al) usually gives a present for all the family." BRONIA.S

"Every year I always wake up the household with Slade's *Merry Christmas Everybody* blaring out on Christmas morning." DAWN.L

*"The whole family goes to the butchers to collect the turkey. We all wear fancy dress. When we get it home each of us slaps it on the bottom twice!"*ALEX.H

"Traditions? No – it's just me and my husband but we always drink Champagne on Christmas Eve if that counts!" YASMIN.W

"Since my Dad was told to give up smoking (he had a stroke), he just has one cigar a year, it is always on Christmas Day." ALEX.P

"I used to look at my Dad's pile and think it was very small and now I'm the Dad and I've got the small pile." RICHARD.U

CHRISTMAS SHOPPING

Mrs.Holford had most of hers
done in November...

CHRISTMAS SHOPPING

When do you start getting ready for Christmas? I now know that as part of their *Normal British Christmas* people start and finish their Christmas shopping at all different times and that for some it's a year-round activity. I'm an early December person myself.

CHRISTMAS SHOPPING

"Jane starts Christmas shopping in January!" ANDREW.B

"I start in the January sales and pick up things throughout the whole year. My husband is more last minute.com and leaves everything to the last day."
TRACY.H

"Last year I went for a sort of Scandinavian vibe with a white tree, white lights adorned with white and silver baubles – most of these were brought in the January Christmas decoration sales! I love a good bargain!"
CHARLOTTE.H

"Some of my family plan Christmas shopping in the January Sales like a military campaign. Armed with lists they know what stores to hit first and who is going

where, with whom and getting what. I'm still in bed when they leave." BRETT.C

"Do my Christmas shopping all year long. I say OMG that's the perfect present for X and I just get it. I have an Aladdin's cave drawer that I keep them all in and I open it closer to Christmas and say oh yes, I remember I bought that for X, sometimes I end up with several presents for one person!" SARA.F

"As a child it used to drive me crazy that on summer holidays, usually Blackpool or Bridlington, my mother would start buying Christmas presents for family and friends as she would see things. We would scream at her as it seemed like this would end summer quicker than we would like. But as the inevitable happens and we become our parents I find myself doing the same now." MICHAEL.K

"From Aug onwards. With my expanding large family I need to start early." MICHELLE.T

"I just go to Waterstones and get books for everyone, all done by the 30/9." NIGEL.R

"I shop from September to November. By December all wrapped and waiting, no stress, I have always done it that way." BARBARA.G

"Some in September when Mum's here so she could take them back and we could avoid postage!" JAN.S

"I tend to do it from September onwards, picking things up when I see them and crafting gifts always takes me a few months!" LAURA.M

"In the 60s it would be shopping on foot trudging round shops whenever I had a spare moment starting sometime in October. Now, shopping on line and from quality magazines. So much easier." JUNE.B

"Last year I started my Christmas shopping at the end of November, I normally start in October, I wasn't as organised as I normally am!" TONI.J

"As for me, I now have a secret weapon (my phone) I have a small folder on it called Presents and Christmas. Each time Polly says 'Oh that's quite nice' I discretely make a note in my folder. Then when it comes to buying

I look at the list, blitz the shops about 10 days before Christmas. Plus online shopping, although I typically leave that too late. So I have the theory, but the execution needs refining." FRANCO.C

"Mrs Holford had most of hers done in November. I did mine during December. Some bits in the weekend before Christmas when I took the boys out to buy a present for Mummy." PETER.H

"Most between Early November and Mid December. I'm incredibly organised and a big control freak, so I love getting them all bought, wrapped and ready early." JEFF.A

THE BILL
£22 billion pounds is spent by British households over the Christmas period each year, with an estimated £634 million pounds being spent on presents.

"Last year I started my Christmas shopping in the middle of November. My aim was to get all my shopping done nice and early however I bought my last Christmas present a few days before the big day. (So my plan didn't turn out very well)." SAM.S

20

"I did mine early December so I had time to wrap them all up." CLAIRE.P

"I usually start thinking about presents early in December and then buy them all at once!" MICAELA.S

"Spread out over all of December." CHRISTOPHER.J

"Start shopping when November arrives and not before." EMMA.R

"I got the rest of the presents the week leading up to Christmas, hated it, credit card went over limit." JAN.S

"Usually in the week before Christmas because I'm horribly disorganised. Last year I achieved a new personal record having bought and wrapped every present by the 23rd!" SAMIRA.S

"It makes me very nervous when Al leaves it all to the last minute but he's been like that for 20+ years and it seems to work." BRONIA.S

"I tend to do all my Christmas shopping in the week running up to Christmas, including panic buying on Christmas Eve." MANDY.R

"I do mine very last minute. I like the Christmas shopping buzz." RACHAEL.H

"Often Christmas Eve – it makes it fun, but scary!" CHARLOTTE.K

"I finished Christmas Eve. I've no idea when my husband did his (he only needed to buy one!)" KAREN.K

"I always still have presents to buy – I call them New Year's Gifts instead." ASH.Y

ADVENT CALENDARS

She fell for it every year...

ADVENT
CALENDARS

Before my research into the *Normal British Christmas* I thought the choice was between a snowy scene Advent calendar or a traditional Nativity one. Now I realise they come in all shapes and sizes and that they don't all contain chocolate!

ADVENT CALENDARS

"We have large handmade numbered Advent pockets that I made, they hang from the spiral staircase and I fill them up with things I've collected for the family all year." CLARA.Y

"Beautiful wooden Advent calendar with compartment big enough for two wee chocolates left by the Christmas fairy. You are not allowed to look ahead otherwise she takes those ones out! Also an Advent calendar with miniature books with Christmas story, each little book is a Christmas decoration that gets added to the tree after each child has read the little book in turn." MANDY.R

"I don't have an Advent calendar, I tend to eat way too much chocolate over Christmas so one extra a day would be lethal!" TONI.J

"No Advent calendar for me but I've got one for my dog Murphy." DAWN.L

"Even though I am arguably too old for an Advent calendar, I get away with it because I share one with my sister. We have a red felt one, with 24 pockets that tie up with little red bows. Mum fills these with different treats every year. The only requirement is chocolate!" NATASHA.W

"As a child yes, often one where you made something each day that contributed to the Nativity Scene, on Christmas Day you added the baby Jesus." GWEN.R

"I always have an Advent Candle. And I light it on the 1st Dec then I get distracted with phone calls or emails and all of a sudden it's the 10th Dec before I remember to blow it out! I have previously burnt it all the way down to 24th Dec in early December! Doh." KEVIN.S

"Bought cheap job at supermarket and put it out to see what Lucy and Sam would do. They gladly devoured the crappy chocolates and even had a system of alternating so it was fair. Felt like a cheapskate, next year will splash out for better one." JAN.S

"As a child I always shared a chocolate one with my sister. I finally confessed to her a few years ago of my guilty secret. I always let my sister open the first day as day 24 used to have a larger chocolate! She fell for it every year. Nowadays I share a chocolate one with my partner and the chocolates are all the same size." TERESA.S

"Sadly not, but did you SEE the one on offer at Liberty? Worth £450 (all beauty products) but sold for £150. It was enormous and sold out I think." NATALIE.J

"We had four. I had a *Minnie Mouse* one, my youngest had a *Spiderman* one, my eldest had *Avengers* & my husband had *One Direction* (that was the only one left in the shop)." CLAIRE.P

"Normally one traditional Nativity and one made of matchboxes with a message or task in each one." RUTH.P

"We had a paper origami-like tree where each day we added a paper decoration on." KATHRYN.J

"Millie and George have chocolate Advent calendars, one at my house and one at their home." BARBARA.G

"A wooden house with 24 drawers for chocolates."
AMANDA.H

"I made one for my husband with pockets in that he had a Bible verse and chocolate in each day. I plan to make one for myself and the baby this year when I (hopefully) have more time!" LISA.C

"Yes, for Daisy and Luke. Same one every year, made out of material with pockets and a star on the end of a ribbon to mark each day. Sweets are placed each night."
FRANCO.C

"I remember a neighbour's kid always had a LEGO calendar, with pieces behind each door. I was always jealous." BRETT.C

WORLD RECORD
St Pancras International station's 2007 Advent Calendar was 71m high and 23m wide. The huge sponsored windows raised money for Great Ormond Street Hospital.

"Yes, I was given a chocolate Advent calendar by my kids as I was working away from home and they thought an Advent calendar was a nice way of reminding me of them, as if I needed reminding!" CHILLY.H

"I remember, as a young child being bought one each year by my Godmother. It always had a nativity scene on it. My sisters were always jealous because they didn't get one and had to make do with a used one from a previous year. The doors on theirs were always popping open before the day arrived!" CATHERINE.M.S

"My 6yr old son, Freddie, dutifully opens the windows when he gets up each morning but doesn't have the chocolate until after school." KEVIN.S

"A friend made a copy of our house, using fretwork, as an Advent calendar and we still use it. (My divorced wife and I are together at Christmas)." PETER.P

"We have a chocolate one for Bruno, still wants one although he is 14." HELEN.H

"Mine is a paper one but I always create 24 individual parcels for my daughter, hubby and Mum and they open them each day. The parcels contain odd things, i.e. Barbie doll shoes. My husband always gets socks." YVONNE.A.S

"No, but we have Advent candles. Four white candles with a red wooden holder and each lit on the Sundays leading up to Christmas." AMY.H

"Had an Advent Calendar as a child and remember a huge battle as to who was going to open each day's door." SARA.F

"Just a milk chocolate one, it was a *Me-To-You Bear* design. I'd bought it for my girlfriend, but she forgot to buy me one so we ended up sharing it!" JEFF.A

"I have the Advent Calendar that my Mum made for myself and my siblings when I was little. It's huge and is a village made out of fabric. Each house is a pocket and Number 24 is a big church in the middle. My kids take turns with it and usually get a chocolate coin, a snowflake to stick on the window and a decoration for a mini Advent tree which goes on the kitchen table!" EMILY.A

"No Advent Calendar, but would love one." ALFRED.W

DECORATIONS

We tried tinsel once, we're still finding bits of it years later...

DECORATIONS

I have discovered people have quite strong views on tinsel – do you love it or loathe it? Do you get five large boxes of decorations down from the attic or prefer to buy new ones? Always have the same colour scheme, or change it every year? Maybe it's only holly and ivy for you, or just old-fashioned paper balls? It's clear each *Normal British Christmas* looks very different on the inside.

DECORATIONS

"Always get tinsel. You don't want that anemic, patchy in a stray dog kind of way tinsel. No, you want lush, fulsome, almost furry, borderline opulent tinsel." JOE.H

"Only gold glass baubles. No tinsel." ANDY.D

"Tinsel everywhere – on bannisters, on curtains, on the fridge." NAJIA.K

"We have our tree decorated with silver and white. No tinsel as I find this can look a bit tacky. The normal lights and baubles." TONI.J

"Tinsel around pictures. Candles on mantlepiece" SALLY.W

"No tinsel. Our cats like to play with the tree enough

and I think tinsel would drive them nuts." KATHRYN.J

"We tried tinsel once, we're still finding bits of it years later." BRETT.C

"Just inside the main entrance is a very precious metal Nativity set (purchased at the Vatican) and bunches of mistletoe hang in both the kitchen and our sitting room." MARTIN.K

"We buy lots of felt, all different colours and we cut out mini stockings and make them into bunting. We hang them everywhere around the house." YANA, AGE 8

"We also made Martha Stewarts 3D snowflakes for our hall (which looked striking)." MICHELLE.T

"Inside talking reindeer and some four-foot metal Nutcracker figures. We love it and so do the kids." TINA.T

"A few 'arty' Santa Clauses on the radiator cover, a large stand up 'Santa Bear' in the hallway." NATASHA.M

"We have a singing polar bear!" LISA.C

"I like to put up as many fairy lights as I can in as many rooms as I can. Paul hates this as there are so many to turn off at bedtime! I also have a Nativity set, a star light on the door and as many other things I can squeeze in." EMILY.A

"My Dad used to put a large paper star over the light bulb in the hall. It was magical." PAUL.S

"Just Christmas cards on mantelpiece and a wooden hedgehog ornament from Germany." STEPHANIE.A

"I have some hand-painted glass decorations, two pears and two doves, I really love getting them out every year." LEIGH.A

"I decorate the large palm tree in the flat and put out the Nativity scene that was made by the secondary boys at the school where I taught so long ago. Mary is both pregnant and holding a baby" MARGARET.H

"Christmas tree branch trimmings around the mirror above the fire place with holly. A small bunch of mistletoe which we pick from a tree locally." FRANCO.C

"A wreath on the bar so I could hear if any of W's friends were breaking into it at his Christmas party in the house. Don't know what I was thinking: G and I were at a restaurant around the corner." NANCY.W

"We have a large pre-lit snowman." CLAIRE.P

"Every year I keep more decorations, this year I filled my 5th box." TINA.K

"Some years ago I knitted a complete Nativity Scene which even had a stable over it, now there is not space in our small cottage so I have donated it to the Village Reception Hall." JOY.B

"Christmas plates, dishes, napkins, tea-towels." ISSY.R

"I brought a mini Ruldolf made from twigs which was very cute." HAYLEY.S

"Some handmade plaster bells and holly shapes covered in glitter and some homemade paper chains. It's all about showing off my daughter's creativity and having fun." TINA.T

"My Godfather, Tony, gave me a tiny clay Nativity set from Italy when I was younger, we still get it out every year." BEN.M

"There are even decorations that I made in Guides when I was 13 above the fireplace." LAURA.M

"I have these exquisite Fabergé type eggs, I open them up and up fill them with tiny LED lights and they look beautiful." SIMON.G

"Always handmade decorations, last year straws covered in wrapping paper with ribbon at each end." SAMANTHA.D

"We have a glass plum Christmas pudding we hang in the bedroom window." KATHYRN.J

"No decorations. I live with two other men who also work in the city and are quite busy and we all go home for Christmas to our family homes." ADAM.L

"We always had mistletoe hung by sellotape from one of the door frames." JOHNNY.M

"Poinsettias in most rooms, a wire reindeer in the hallway." AUDREY.H

"Inside we went back to old school with the paper balls of various sizes and a reindeer display in the hall." PETE.B

"My plaster Nativity is very old and was given to us by a neighbour, it must date back to the 1930s." ANNE.P

"I have a wonderful chandelier which I love adding coloured glass decorations to." MICHAEL.K

"I bought some nice unusual lights, plastic balls in colorful knitted covers" NIKA.G

"On the dining table we have a centre piece of fir branches and other evergreens, which is also home to the first cloved orange we make each year." NATASHA.W

"My Mum has a Snowman in the kitchen that she adds a 'special thing' to each year of something

that happened within the year, he only comes out for Christmas." CHARLOTTE.H

"I have a live mini tree and decorations are hundreds of tiny red satin bows on hair pins that I made for my Mum in 1975. I store them in a small tin and it comes out every year." SARA.F

"Favourite decorations are homemade blown eggs, sprayed silver/gold and covered in glitter and painted ones by Mum & Dad from when we were kids." REBECCA.S

"We have a beautiful porcelain Nativity set that takes centre stage. And one of those lovely candle-driven rotating ornaments from the German market." BRONIA.S

"I have garlands on my stairs, hanging decorations for the windows, assorted ornaments and a little faux tree next to my fish tank." TERESA.S

"Christmas bunting (with the individual letters that spell Christmas stitched onto each triangle) hung from the mantlepiece." SAM.S

"We are keen skiers so some of the decorations were bought in France, of skiers and the like." PAM.T

"Glimmery snowflakes on curtains." MARGO.F

"Lighted white star hanging in window." AMY.H

"Last year found some cool paper chains, I haven't done these and streamers since I was a kid, I used to love them." REBECCA.S

"We have a small modern triangular red cone with internal lights inside." SALLY-ANNE.E

"A puppet my Grandson made when he was little, *Christmas Pudding Man*, hangs in a doorway." JOAN.D

"I always wanted the candles in the window, I think my Dad thought it was a waste of electricity!" TASNEEM.K

"Subversively the garage is full of decorations before Christmas. My partner has no idea, then they just appear overnight and she has to deal with it. She can't be Humbug, they're up." OLIVER.G

OUTSIDE

Douglas risked his life ...

OUTSIDE

How we present the *Normal British
Christmas* to the outside is one thing
that everyone can see, whether it's
a display that challenges the national
grid or a discreet festive wreath. I was
horrified when my husband and son
put an ancient sheep's skull on the
front door with a red bauble on its
nose. They christened it *Rudolph
the Dead Nose Reindeer.*

OUTSIDE

"We have reindeers that light up on the roof and a jolly Father Christmas. More lights hanging from the trees."
KIERON.D

"We have a Father Christmas climbing out of the window." SAMI, AGE.7

"Wreath on the door. No big outdoor illuminations or Santa coming out of the Chimney!" FRANCO.C

"I always have the most deluxe proper wreath - dried oranges, cinnamon sticks and holly sprigs." SARA.F

"A large wooden star on the front door made out of painted twigs." JEFF.A

"Outside I help my Grandparents put up a wreath by the door, a large lighted star over the garage, lights in the shape of a tree over the big front window, two lighted spiral trees, and lots of other lights and garlands. It's a lot of work, but it always ends up looking very nice and tasteful." BRETT.C

"In our courtyard we have a large illuminated metal reindeer and a simple holly wreath on one of the entrance doors." MARTIN.K

"We have some small white lights in the bamboo plants." PETER.H

"Douglas risked his life to adorn the house with twinkling icicle lights (white), as well as on our old apple tree in the garden." MICHELLE.T

"We have a massive palm tree on our front lawn that we decorated with lights and extra-large Christmas Baubles." DEBRA.W

"We have some inflatable snowmen and Father Christmas figures that we place outside." PATRICK.M

"Nothing outside, my husband keeps giving me gloomy statistics about the 15 people killed each year putting up their external Christmas decorations!" GEMMA.L

"As we arrived at Centre Parcs with my Aunt and Uncle we saw a man thoroughly stapling fake snow onto every surface. He looked very, very tired. The next morning we awoke to real thick snow everywhere. We laughed and cried for the man that night." BEN.M

"We had lights in one of the trees in the garden as well as hanging icicle lights under the eaves." TRACY.H

"I acquired a tinsel Santa face and put this on the door. Also, for the first time ever, bought Christmas doormats – I didn't want to wipe my feet on them before entering the house as they looked so nice!" CHILLY.H

"It gets very competitive between the streets in this area, who has the most trees with lights in. I was delighted the year we won." PAT.M

"I had a wreath on my door and fairy lights in the planters outside my flat." CHARLOTTE.H

"A thing on the door that says NOEL." AMANDA.H

"We have a two-foot Santa at the front door." DIANE.G

"Nothing modern, no lights – just a wreath on the front door, looks amazing on my old Georgian front door." BARBARA.G

"A holly wreath on the front door plus a sign saying Please Stop here Santa!" KEVIN.S

"Door wreath of dried red berries." ANDY.D

"My Mum puts a robin on top of the gate." TIM, AGE.9

"We always have a festive wreath on the door. We've taken to making our own the last few years." NATASHA.W

"By the time I remembered the wreath for the front door Christmas was over!" NADINE.A

THE TREE

Our angel is the ugliest in the world...

THE TREE

What's your point of view on white lights versus coloured lights? I was talking to Jamie from *Smiths Salon* about this debate (he's my colourist, there's a lot of time to talk). "Mark and I don't have any rules about lights," he told me, "We just always have the normal non-coloured ones."

THE TREE

"The biggest question of your book must be white lights or coloured lights. White of course!" PATRICK.S

"Have coloured lights. Lots of chocolates too (as they mysteriously disappear – I think Santa's elves keep returning every night!)" CHILLY.H

"We were sent outside on Christmas Eve and when we came back in the tree was decorated with real candles, all lit up. It was so beautiful it took your breath away." JIM.M

"Buried somewhere amongst all the decorations our tree has a mixture of white and coloured lights." ISSY.R

"I had a miniature real Christmas tree, I made tiny white snowflakes which hung from the branches." STEPHANIE.A

"The biggest tree we had was huge, my 6ft Dad had to stand on a box on a table to reach the top." SIMON.G

"Yes, I did have a Christmas tree, all seven-foot-three inches of it! The tree is so tall that the star placed on top is bent forward due to it touching the ceiling." SAM.S

"We have a pre-lit artificial tree and we decorate it in silver and turquoise to match our sitting room. The tree is decorated by me & the kids." CLAIRE.P

"We always got our tree from Columbia Road Flower Market, then we'd go to the Nelson's Head and park it in the corner while we had a drink. Then we'd watch as the corner of the pub gradually filled up with Christmas trees." JAMIE.S

"I have a tiny Christmas Tree (maybe 10-15cm tall) and although the tree is over 12 years old, I love it, because I still remember the day we bought it with my Mum. Because of the size of my Christmas tree, I love to say that my presents are not under the tree, but the tree is on top of the presents." INDRE.G

"Our Christmas tree was so high it reached the ceiling. Papa was in charge of decorating it and my brother and I helped. We used to cover the tree in a sort of material we called 'Angel Hair'." MICAELA.S

"It's always real candles on our tree, it's something my Mum always insisted on." ORLANDO.J

"We use the same Christmas tree each year. My parents put it up this year around mid-December, decorated with new red and gold baubles, some beads (which I really do hate) and twinkling white lights to top it off!" SAMIRA.S

"Last year we had a tiny tree, next to my new granddaughter, with old trimmings and lights." PETER.P

"The tree last year was gorgeous, but really heavy and crooked. It fell over two days after we put it up!" NANCY.W

"I have to admit I get little bit emotional around Christmas as always reminds me of my Dad, because when I was little me and him always did the tree together." JASMINA.J

"Everyone in the whole town has a minature real tree displayed above their front door." MAUREEN.B

"Christmas in the barn and the fun of getting the biggest tree we could find in there, it eventually became ridiculous with a 25ft (and very heavy) tree strapped onto the roof of a difficult to steer and rather erratic Jeep." ROBIN.P

"Ash, from Home Care DIY, goes to Norway and Poland every year and chooses 2,000 trees to bring back. You can wander around and take your time choosing then stand around the coal brazier, listening to Christmas music while he and his sister Bharti put it in a net. It's great. They deliver it to you the same day." FRANCES.S

"We have two trees (one for each sitting room) and both real. A bit of an annual ritual as my wife insists the tree has to 'look like a tree from top to bottom' so takes ages getting them all out of the nets to make her selection!" MARTIN.K

"Don't have a real tree (too uneven!) Decorated by all of us, perfected by me." NATASHA.M

"Went out and got a real Christmas tree on the morning of 13th December. Took it home and levelled the bottom of it with a saw and it took two of us to get it indoors and into a holder and up straight." CHILLY.H

THANK YOU TREE
Every year Norway sends a 20m Christmas tree to London's Trafalgar Square. The gift is to thank the British people for our help in World War II.

"Our tree lives in a pot in the garden and comes in every year from about mid-December and goes out again around 12th night. Surprisingly this doesn't seem to kill it. This year it had red baubles and red reindeer and white lights – decorated by me." GEMMA.L

"Our expensive artificial tree has lasted a number of years. I am too environmental to agree with chopping down a real tree just to put in the front room." MICHELLE.T

"Best Christmas tree buying experience? The farmer took us to his field, got out his chainsaw and said which one do you want? He cut it down there and then." JOHNNY.M

"Growing up we always had a real tree, it was a family tradition to all go and buy it together. We had the same decorations each year. Today we have a fake tree but I change the decorations each year in themes (this year it's red)." MICHAEL.K

"As I live alone, I don't bother with a proper tree. I have a two-foot silver tree-shaped decoration which is covered in glitter that I have used in place of a tree for the last few years. I hang a couple of baubles on it and it looks quite cute. In fact, I have three baubles now!" ROSE.Y

"We had a real Christmas tree that although bought here in London was grown in Poland. (I'm Polish, my husband is British). We decorated it together with our five-year old daughter with baubles, cinnamon sticks and gingerbread decorations (made in Poland)." NIKA.G

"We have an artificial tree. My other half and my son decorate the tree, I point! Always looks lovely with vintage wooden tree decorations, some coloured baubles and static white lights, plus this year a crystal snowflake at the top." KEVIN.S

"My Mum decorates our real tree with long silver bits that drape over the branches. A friend asked her where she got them. She told her she didn't remember as she had bought them about 10 years ago. 'You keep them?' the friend asked in amazement. I can confirm she does, every year she makes us remove and pack them all up, every single piece!" SOPHIE.S

"We have the same good quality artificial tree, red and gold baubles, beads and tinsel that we bought in John Lewis on our first Christmas. A mixture of white and coloured lights, individual hanging decorations (gifts from friends and children that I've taught), chocolates, gold bows and a gold star at the top." AUDREY.H

"I have an artificial tree. Lots of lights, very old sentimental ornaments from my childhood, I have some as old as me. Mainly Victorian style, Joe gave me one from America, that an old Indian squaw made for him, and a Crown from Westminster Abbey." BARBARA.G

"We have a scrawny Father Christmas made of pipe cleaners that goes on the top of the tree." SOPHIE.S

"The top is ALWAYS a star. This year I used the star my Dad always used. I decorate the tree with the help of my younger son." ANNE.P

"Our angel on top of the tree was made with wires, tinsel and stocking wool by Georgia when she was 6 (now 23) with a SA friend of mine - our angel is the ugliest in the world." MANDY.R

"We have a naked angel on top of our tree, she lost her clothes about 15 years ago." JOAN.B

"The Christmas tree is the centrepiece for us. We take the art direction quite seriously! Chris, the only man the house, tends to just stay out of the way and makes sustaining cups of tea. We usually play vintage Christmas carols while we decorate, just to make sure everyone is suitably in the Christmas spirit." NATASHA.W

"I hate decorating the Christmas tree – but I hate it even more if they do it without me." ERIC.S

SECRET SANTA

Now they tell me about the poem!

SECRET SANTA

"I can't believe it," fumed my son Ben, arriving home with the sparkly candle holder. "No swapping?! Don't they know there's only one way to do Secret Santa?!" Turns out there are lots of ways — I wonder if I've found the version you do?

SECRET SANTA

"For Secret Santa we sit in a circle and go around clockwise with everyone choosing a present when it's their turn. You can swap the present if you don't like it."
BEN.M

"For Secret Santa we sit in a circle and go in alphabetical order to pick prizes. No swapping."
MELANIE.F

"You email if you want to join the work Secret Santa, adding a profile with three of your interests. Names get drawn from a virtual hat and we hand them out at the pub." WILLIAM.R

"Secret Santa for us is you buy a silly present, the more ridiculous the better. Number 1 can choose a present,

then number 2 can either choose a new present, or take number 1's, with Number 1 having to chose a new present. It becomes a massive negotiation, utter chaos, people are screaming 'take mine, take mine'. There's always one thing that gets traded over and over again, last year it was the Downton Abbey pencil case." GAVIN.S

"In our Secret Santa we buy gifts around £10 and, because we all like each other, everyone tries to get something nice." KYLA.T

"For the adults in the family we do a Secret Santa where everyone chooses something they want for up to £100. I keep a list and give everybody a present to buy. Everyone gets one £100 present rather than lots of small things they may not want. (We all still buy for all the kids)." DIANE.E.G

"Every year we have different criteria for how you pick a prize in our Secret Santa with the neighbours. Last time it was tallest to smallest (tallest went first.)" JIM.M

"After my parents got divorced, we'd spend Christmas Eve with my Dad's side of the family and Christmas

day with my Mum's. At my Dad's everyone would draw names for a 'Secret Santa' – it meant that we all got a mystery gift on top of everything else." BRETT.C

"Now we are doing Secret Santa in the family which isn't secret at all, because you find out who has your name and drop very large hints as to what you would like." MARGARET.H

"My Secret Santa at work this year, I hated it! At the last minute they told me they each write a poem about the person you were buying the present for and why the present you got suited them – but I'd just joined and got someone I didn't know very well. "Now they tell me about the poem" I thought! On the day the manager read all the poems out one by one! Some were really witty and everyone laughed, but mine was terrible and no-one laughed." CAROLINE.M

"This year was different for me as I was at my new in-law's house. We did Secret Santa with 26 family members and with the aid of an excited two-year old to help everyone unwrap their presents." TASNEEM.K

"I like taking part in an internet Secret Santa. You get a name of someone you don't know and send to someone you don't know, everyone is in the UK. The girl who sent me a present included a Christmas card." BEN.M

"Our Secret Santa at work only starts off secret. You pull someone's name out of the hat and then have to buy a present for them. We have a set amount to spend. Nobody knows who has bought for who, until we get to the pub and people start dropping hints. By the end of the night everyone knows everything!" MAUREEN.B

BAUBLES

Our tree is a story book ...

BAUBLES

Is your tree a story book? This evocative phrase that *Debra.W* uses sums up what so many people said. Whether it's the baubles that have been collected over the lifetime of the family, or the comfort and joy that comes from returning to the familiar, each *Normal British Christmas* is clearly a story that is passed on through the generations.

CHRISTMAS BAUBLES

"Real Christmas tree with baubles, old ones which we bought a long time ago and special ones given as gifts over the years, usually colour-coordinated." SALLY.W

"Every year we buy something new for the tree. Last year, as it was the first Christmas me and my boyfriend were living together, my Mum bought us Mr & Mrs Claus baubles with our names on them." SAM.S

"We always have chocolate baubles, most get eaten before Christmas (when no one's looking) but a few survive to be devoured when the decorations come down." RICH.S

"We have a proper chest of hand-painted baubles that my Nan bought, we take them out every year." NATHAN.A

"The decorations have all been bought in other countries – we got our first one in Disneyland – and some of our glass baubles are from when we first got married." JANE.B

"My Mum fills a glass vase with my brother and I's childhood special baubles." CHARLOTTE.H

"My daughter had a small tree to decorate as she pleased. She had baubles and a King Henry VIII decoration." TINA.T

"I also painted a bauble of a night snow scene!" PAM.T

"The Christmas Tree Fairy delivers the tree. We write a letter to the fairy asking her to bring us a tree and letting her know if we want to decorate it ourselves. This is my husband's family tradition but one that the children love. We do it on the evening of the 10th Dec as my husband's father passed away on 11th so it is something nice to do on that day. We have an artificial tree which is delivered

VICTORIAN BALLS
Christmas 1832, Queen Victoria wrote of her delight about having a decorated tree. A newspaper photograph of her tree decorated with glass balls started our love of baubles.

by the Christmas Tree Fairy (see below) on the evening of 10th Dec. We have white lights, tinsel and baubles. The main colours are gold and purple however we have a few 'special' baubles that are different. The tree can be decorated by the fairy or you can ask her to leave the decorations for us to do, last year this happened and all four of us did it together." HANNAH.M

"My sister and I get to choose a new decoration every year, Mummy buys it and it goes in the box. Two days before Christmas we put everything in the box on the tree, if we did it earlier things might get knocked off." ANNABEL, AGE.9

"Every year when we decorate the tree I buy our kids a new ornament that is symbolic of what they are into that year. Our tree is a story book, a beautiful chaotic display of our lives." DEBRA.W

"Yes, always had a tree and we all 'helped' to decorate it. Plenty of baubles old and new, some of our school made decorations that gradually got tattier as the years passed, and if we were well-behaved we were allowed chocolate decorations." TERESA.S

"My sisters always come over to our home to help me dress the tree (hooray!) We sing (loudly and badly) to Christmas music and drink wine (mulled)!" JULIANNA.G

"I always get out my same decorations every year as they bring back lots of happy memories. Some of these decorations were made by my (now grown up) children when they were at nursery and later school. I do always try to pick up a Christmas decoration when I go on holiday and this again brings back great memories of places visited." CHILLY.H

"The kids school-made decorations have been gracefully retired after many years' service." BRONIA.S

"Children given instructions to put tree up in my absence one day – Sam's method: put basic tree together. Take all baubles and tinsel and throw at said tree to see where they land. Forget to put star on top as too busy needing to go play a PS4 game. Suffice to say I fixed it up when the kids were asleep." JAN.S

"Some of my decorations are over 30 years old, I don't like it if there's a single undecorated branch." TINA.K

"Spread across our Christmas tree are some exquisite hand-beaded baubles that my Nana makes. Every year she gives us new ones." BEN.M

"I like the idea of the kids helping but then have to move the decorations they put up as they make it asymmetrical." LEIGH.A

"Our tree goes up on Dec 1st, decorations are all red, the same as both my parent's & grandparent's trees." SAM.S

"About three weeks before Christmas, we ALWAYS play Nat King Cole and that signals the start for us. Polly does a beautiful tree with the kids, whilst I sort and untangle the lights. No tinsel, but lots of red ribbon bows, glass baubles and tiny gold wrapped boxes, red and white theme with silver and red pearl strings." FRANCO.C

"Our tree goes up 12 days before Christmas and there is always a colour theme (we have literally 100s of baubles). My husband decorates the tree (he is a strapping MUFC supporter but decorates the most beautiful tree)." TRACY.H

"We always wait until 16th December (which was the date we got it when I was growing up) and decorate the same day with lights, tinsel and anything in the Christmas decoration box." CHARLOTTE.K

"We put ours up about five to seven days before Christmas and decorate with with lights, one string of tinsel and wooden, felt and plastic baubles." HELEN.H

"Tree in the living room decorated on Christmas Eve (not before). Small wax baby Jesus in manger with glass baubles and birds, tinsel, real candles in holders. Real candles! What was I thinking? Now, electric!" JUNE.B

"We got our tree the weekend before Christmas but that is normal. It was decorated with everything we had, looked like a circus. Hahahaha. January, it's still up." JASMINA.J

HIDING PRESENTS

It's really quite difficult to get a bike up into a loft...

HIDING PRESENTS

Some people hide presents, some don't. I know (and I'm sure by now you also know) that with the *Normal British Christmas* there's no point in starting a sentence with '*surely the right way is*' or '*nobody does that*' because for someone it isn't and somebody does.

HIDING PRESENTS

"Presents are hidden at the North Pole until they arrive down the chimney on Christmas Day. Santa helpfully divides them into piles for each person." GEMMA.L

"They used to hide the presents. My sister always found them beforehand but I never did and she would never tell me where they were." PETER.B

"My Mum and Dad hid all the presents in the loft, one year that included a bike. Impressive. It's really quite difficult to get a bike into the loft you know." SIMON.G

"When our kids were little I used to hide the presents in my wardrobe, the kids were clueless. Now they have to be locked up in the garage as they are better at looking for them (and taller!)" LEIGH.A

"I hid my husband's present at my Mum and Dad's house, partly so he didn't find it, partly so I didn't snap and give it to him early and ruin the surprise!" TASNEEM.K

"We were relentless hounds and would look in every spot for hidden presents. We found them loads of times – left them of course and then showed complete surprise on Christmas day – easy really as you never knew who it was for when you found a gift – could be any one of the four of you!" SARA.F

"By December I have a treasure trove of bits and bobs hidden away that I really look forward to giving!" NATASHA.W

"I have to hide them as my daughter won't leave them alone and guesses what she has got!" LAURA.B

"I stuff things away all year (all hidden in different places) everyone gets a lot more that way!" COLLETTE.B

"I buy presents throughout the year, always hoping that I will remember where I've stored all the gifts!" TINA.T

CHRISTMAS EVE

It's time for the new pyjamas ...

CHRISTMAS EVE

Is your Christmas Eve a mad-dash day?
Or are you snuggling up with a movie by
early afternoon? I found lots of seasonal
cooking happening, lots of travelling –
people spoke of crowded trains full of
passengers, presents spilling out of bags. I
heard tales of frantic shopping and
last-minute wrapping while others
were enjoying a day of candle-lit
calm. Church services and
Christmas Carols
for many.

CHRISTMAS EVE

"When it's time for The New Pyjamas I am so excited I think I will explode." STEPHEN, AGE.6

"I always cook a red wine casserole for Christmas Eve, it takes ages but it's worth it." JOAN.D

"My husband and I always lock the doors early on Christmas Eve and enjoy a seafood platter and a bottle of Laurent Perrier Rose. Pure heaven!" TRACY.H

"On Christmas Eve in the late afternoon Santa delivers a package to our doorstep containing new PJs, a film and some hot chocolate. There is a note in there saying something along the lines of 'I know you are very excited so here are some things to help you sleep'. We then give them a bath, put their new PJs on and sit

and watch the film with the hot chocolate, although the children never drink theirs! Not sure if it helps them to settle down or not, but we like it!" HANNAH.M

"I make a *Baileys* and *Nutella* cheescake with a nice wheat-free base. It has to be *Baileys* or it wouldn't feel like Christmas, would it?!" LOTTIE.M

"We always get a pair of Crimbo PJ's, this year mine had Christmas pugs!" SALLY-ANNE.E

"Despite us being 27 and 31, Mum still buys us new PJs for Christmas Eve" AGNETA.R

"Every Christmas Eve we all watch a Christmas movie in our new pjs, then we stay in them till Boxing Day!" SAMANTHA.D

"On Christmas Eve it's tree decorating listening to the *Ceremony of Carols* on Radio 3. Then we have the Fish Pie, that's something that everyone has isn't it?" RUTH.P

"We always have fish pie on Christmas Eve, before going to Midnight Mass together." ANGELA.F

"It has to be Maison Bertaux Mince Pies for us." TIM.S

"We begin on Christmas Eve with M&S nibbles and then a takeaway." CHARLES.K

"We always do 'The Donkey' on Christmas Eve, our local church's Nativity procession with carol singing outside the church, whatever the weather." MANDY.R

"I light candles in glass candle holders and place them on the doorstep on Christmas Eve to greet us as we return home from the early evening Carol Service."
AUDREY.H

"On Christmas Eve friends of the family come round and we all have mince pies and mulled wine (my Mum makes both). Then we always watch *The Snowman* and if Raymond Briggs' *Father Christmas* is on we watch that too. Then my parents go to Midnight Mass."
RICH.S

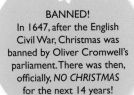

BANNED!
In 1647, after the English Civil War, Christmas was banned by Oliver Cromwell's parliament. There was then, officially, *NO CHRISTMAS* for the next 14 years!

"My sister always makes me rum truffles and presents these to me with aplomb on Crimbo Eve." SALLY-ANNE.E

"Once everything is done and before the Father Christmas tracking starts we we all sit down and watch *It's A Wonderful Life* together. I cry every time." JULIANNA.G

"I have to watch The Polar Express and every year I buy a new bauble that says I Believe." LOTTIE.M

"We always watch *Muppets Christmas Carol* on Christmas Eve, always." LAURA.M

"Because Advent is a fast time, it's wonderful to have that first mouthful of something sweet and alcoholic. After mass on Christmas Eve, we may have a choccy or mince pie with roast chestnuts and mulled wine." ANNE.P

"We stay at my sister's. On Christmas Eve my Dad comes over and I go and have two pints with him then my brother-in-law and I go and get plastered. In the early AM I have a hangover and my sister's three kids wake me shouting "it's time to open the sacks!" (which are pillowcases)." DOM.D.V

FATHER CHRISTMAS

Talcum powder & elaborate plans
to catch Santa ...

FATHER CHRISTMAS

In my research on the *Normal British Christmas* I found a clear *Yes* and *No* camp when it came to leaving things out for Father Christmas and Rudolph. Then, in the *Yes* camp, there was such a wide variety of exactly what was left out, followed by the question of whether it was eaten or not. Only one thing was certain — everybody knew their answer was the correct one.

FATHER CHRISTMAS

"We make some 'snowy' footprints on the front room and stair carpet before going to bed to show Freddie that Father Christmas has actually been. I used talcum powder last year as I'd run out of flour! It's great having a six-year old that still believes!" KEVIN.S

"Every year I would come up with an elaborate way to catch Father Christmas. One year I recorded my voice onto a cassette saying 'Wake up David! Wake Up David!' Then I made an intricate string arrangement that would trip Father Christmas over and trigger a weight, which would precisely lower down to turn on the cassette recorder, which would then play the message. Sadly, it was another year when I didn't wake up until the morning, I think Father Christmas must have stepped over the string." DAVID.H

"Sleep never came naturally on Christmas Eve, only out of sheer excited exhaustion/terror at the thought of not getting any Christmas presents if we actually saw him." ROBIN.P

"My Dad used to say that Father Christmas came to our house last in the morning. So in the morning we'd hear my Dad say 'Good to see you!' followed by 'Bye, bye' and the door slamming. Dad would shout 'he's been' and we'd all get up." KATE.G

"All presents are from Father Christmas (FC) regardless of age of child/person or whether believe or not!" MANDY.R

"Since Francesca was five we have been abroad for Christmas. The story goes that Father Christmas knows and delivers the presents to the hotel." CATHERINE M.S

"Do we leave anything out for Father Christmas? Yes. Normally we leave a carrot, mince pie and glass of whisky. All of which gets sampled. The kids loved it when they were young and still do!" BRONIA.S

"Yes, he has a pint of lager and a mince pie" KIERON.D

"Yes, a glass of milk and a big slice of Christmas cake."
LLOYD.H

"No, that would be impossible, the dog would beat him to it." KAREN.K

"A mince pie and Ribena." AMANDA.H

"Yes, Santa gets sherry and a mince pie. Occasionally he's had to make do with beer and a digestive biscuit."
JULIANNA.G

"No he's much too fat as it is." JAN.S

"Of course – some parsnip (no carrots available), some spinach – my sister in law is very healthy." GEMMA.L

"Yes, a carrot, glass of milk and a mince pie. Santa cleaned it all off." MICHELLE.T

"I used to leave out a mince pie for Santa but haven't done so for many years. He never ate it!" AUDREY.H

"Mince pie and sherry (despite my assertion that I believed that Father Christmas actually prefers single malt)." PETER.H

"We left some milk and a gingerbread reindeer our daughter had made for Santa. She also drew a picture for him. Santa left a letter saying thank you!" NIKA.G

"We do leave sherry and a mince pie and a sausage roll for Santa. We also leave the bottle out – which one year he finished off!" CHILLY.H

"Millie and George left a drink and a cupcake and a carrot." BARBARA.G

"Sadly, Father Christmas will find no treats for him in our house." SAMIRA.S

"Brandy for Father Christmas, milk for helpers, carrots and mince pies, one of each for each reindeer. Only crumbs left in the morning." AMBER.K

"We never did, he must have gone hungry in our house!"
REBECCA S

"The plate and glass were always the first things my sister and I would check after waking up. Usually it was just crumbs and an empty glass, but I remember the year 'Santa' left us a note saying how much he and his reindeer enjoyed the treats and we were SO excited."
BRETT.C

"Yes, for Father Christmas we leave biscuits, milk and a key (!) as we don't have a chimney but we leave it inside, he's that clever!" SAMANTHA D

"No, Santa is on a diet." STEVE.Y

"As a child, yes. Mince pie and sherry. Interestingly they were always gone in the morning. My grandfather was virtually tee-total so goodness knows who had the sherry – maybe it went back into the bottle! By the way, I did have a father, but my grandfather was Father Christmas and I was very close to him." GWEN.R

"My parents used to scatter half bitten carrots in the garden to claim the reindeers had been, we loved searching the garden for them!." CHARLOTTE.H

"When I was little I always used to leave out a minced pie and a glass of brandy for Father Christmas as well as a carrot for Rudolph. Later on in life my Mum told me that when I would go to bed my Step Dad would eat the minced pie and drink the brandy and my Mum would put the carrot back in the fridge." SAM.S

"One year I was convinced I heard Santa coming up the stairs to thank me for the mince pies, in hindsight it was probably my Dad going to bed." TASNEEM.K

"For Father Christmas I always left a mince pie out, even when they didn't believe. Eventually they said, Mum, get over it – we know you eat it!" COLLETTE.B

WRAPPING PAPER

Everything in a similar shade of beige...

WRAPPING PAPER

The first surprise for me here
was people having a specific
wrapping paper for each person. The
second was people not wrapping
anything at all. "That's the beauty,"
one fan of the unwrapped told me,
"you can see what Father Christmas
has left straightaway." It'll never
catch on in our house.

WRAPPING PAPER

"The door of the front room remains unopened until after breakfast, then Dad peeks in to check if Father Christmas has been. He always has. Each person has a chair in the front room piled high with presents, all unwrapped." JOE.O

I have been experimenting with marbling paper in our bath, so all the presents will be wrapped with that. MARGARET.H

"I like to buy decent quality paper. I bought several different types and pretty patterned string. I don't enjoy shopping much but I really love wrapping gifts." AYLA.P

Wrapping paper – everything a similar shade of beige this year. NATALIE.J

"My Dad will sometimes ask me to wrap his presents, I can do it so that Mum just about believes he's done it himself. One year though he asked Grandma to do it, she has a very regimented approach (straight lines, perfect corners) fused with artistic flair (coordinating colours, curling ribbons with knives). They looked beautiful. Mum knew straightaway he didn't wrap them." JESS.H

"I am not an enthusiastic wrapper, but my boyfriend is a right little elf. I came home to see him curling ribbon and covered in glitter. He does most of mine and my neighbour wrapped his from me. We put them all under the tree. Where else?" KATHRYN.J

"When I was an art student in my late teens, I requested that my presents be wrapped as brown paper parcels like from *The Sound of Music*." ROSE.Y

"I tend to coordinate the wrapping of my Christmas presents with the colour scheme of the tree each year. So as soon as they're wrapped, decorated, and adorned with ribbon, mini baubles, and last year mini-candy canes, the presents become part of the decorations." NATASHA.W

"The BIG PRESENT from Father Christmas would appear on Christmas morning. Not wrapped, just sitting on top of a pile of other stuff you wanted (also not wrapped) with a big handwritten label with your name on - it made it so exciting as you could see immediately what you'd got. We'd all play with these things straight away. That's the way it always was." JOHNNY.M

"Two seven-foot Christmas trees! Presents given to us were displayed under one tree and the presents we bought were displayed under the other tree, all wrapped in silver paper." SALLY-ANNE.E

"My Mum wraps each present in a different kind of paper, always in colours and designs that she thinks we'll like. Part of the fun is seeing how many different ones she has found." MICHAEL.D

"My Mum would always wrap up four bars of soap and some boxes of chocolates with no name on the packages, in case we had surprise visitors. If we didn't, the soap would get unwrapped and go back in the cupboard and we'd get to eat the chocolates." PETER.B

"Everyone has their own colour wrapping paper and we do decorations to match."
SAMANTHA.D

"I try to use one colour wrapping paper for each person but last year I ran out and had to compromise."
CHRISTOPHER.J

"My presents would be badly wrapped if it wasn't for my Mother, I'm a terrible wrapper. She always refuses to do it for me (at first) but eventually gives in and takes over."
RICH.S

"We don't wrap presents, or do surprises. I tell her what I want and she tells me and we just get it for each other and hand it over." HENRY.P

"What my mother forgot to tell you was that she opened all of our presents with a razor blade so that she could find out what was inside, and then took ages carefully sellotaping and wrapping them back together again so that we would never know… she is very nosey around presents and simply has to know what they are, she cannot wait!" ROBIN.P

"Our wrapping paper matches our colour scheme, silver and red this year." STEPHANIE.E

"I always wrap up stocking stuff as it makes it last longer." SALLY.W

"The best bit is wrapping all the gifts, when they're all done I put them under the tree and take a photo." LESLEY.J

"Wherever possible gift bags as I hate wrapping presents." DIANE.G

"Presents all under the tree two or three days before Christmas. All beautifully wrapped with a ribbon and bow and the paper is plain with no patterns, the bows make a big difference." FRANCO.C

"We don't put labels on gifts for each other but label gifts for visitors." AUDREY.H

"My friend's daughter, who had just learnt to read, got up in the night and unwrapped all her presents with her name on – she left the others – "Mummy isn't it great, I can read my own name," she said. My friend cried."
LESLEY.J

"We love wrapping gifts together and always reuse old tags from years ago when William was small." NANCY.W

"Gifts from friends go under the tree, but every year Mum leaves mine unwrapped on the chair in the living room when I'm in bed." LAURA.M

"When my Grandson was two he loved unwrapping the presents much more than any of the gifts themselves. So, the whole day was us re-wrapping presents and him unwrapping them all over again." JOAN.D

"I am usually wrapping presents in the early hours of Christmas Day." FABIENNE.H

CHRISTMAS STOCKINGS

The nail stays up all year...

CHRISTMAS STOCKINGS

Do you have stockings? Pillowcases? Or even submarine socks? As people mentioned pillowcases (and lots did) all I could think was wow, a whole pillowcase! Do they fill it all or just use a corner of it? This was another new concept for me, we've always been a stockings with your name on family ourselves.

CHRISTMAS STOCKINGS

"As kids we had to wait to open the stockings until it was light, otherwise they'd disappear. So when you woke up you'd just look at them for ages until the light came. We never ever did open them early." PENNY.H

"I always remember the amazing feeling in the morning when the weight on the end of the bed had changed. A heavy pressure on my feet was my first inkling that Santa had been." ANNE.P

"Phil's family used black tights as stockings, they had presents in both legs so you'd wake up with these misshapen legs draped over the end of your bed. And Phil's Mum always filled them in the dark, so as people were unwrapping she'd start shouting and grab things back and give them to someone else." CAROLYN.W

"We have two identical stockings for each child. We fill them ahead of time, hide them and the others go on the beds. Once the children are asleep, we swap them, easy to do it in the dark!" SHERYL.B

"Stockings go at the end of the bed, and yes – they are red with our names on! When Gracie was little we used to have to put her stocking in the lounge or in our room, she didn't want Father Christmas in her room, sensible child!" EMILY.A

"Stockings by the fire. This year was the first year the kids waited until their Mum and Dad woke up." RICHARD.S

"We hung our stockings by the fireplace at night and in the morning they be in our room, stuffed full!" FRANCES.S

"Stockings. Hung on the door knobs outside the bedrooms of course!" KEITH.F

"My stocking goes on a nail at the end of my bed. The nail stays up all year, sometimes I catch myself on it but I don't mind, it means I know that Christmas is always coming back again." ANNABEL, AGE.9

"We had stockings in the bedroom and could open them when we woke up, my sister would wake up really early and open hers, and then go back to sleep!" GARETH.M

"We had football socks with a thick comic rolled up in to make a tube, inside was always a tangerine and assorted things collected by Mum throughout the year." DAVID.H

"On our beds, all house guests have one. Dad's old submarine socks." RUTH.P

"The stocking was a pillowcase (and still is for our kids). When I met David I was surprised that Father Christmas wrapped up the things in the stockings and I was also surprised his Mum and Dad had stockings, in our house it was only the children." PENNY.H

"My husband got a MUFC stocking by the side of his bed on Christmas morning as did I (mine had a fairy on it)." SALLY-ANNE.E

"In our stockings we all used to get a selection box, with sweets and chocolate inside and a game on the back, I loved those." JOHNNY M

"As a child, I used my Great-Grandfather's knitted stocking. He was a sea captain and it was in thick, cream wool. The toes/heels were darned. It seemed HUGE, but I don't expect it was. My Grandfather packed it tight, tight with all kinds of stuff. There was always an orange in it. I used to wake up very early (excited, so excited!) and open the stocking. It was tied very, very tightly at the top with twine. All done to keep me quiet and occupied I'm sure." GWEN.R

"There were three stockings on the ottoman next to the fire in the sitting room. They are beautiful handmade padded and lined stockings with traditional Christmas designs. They were filled with toys and snacks, the large one for our dog and the two smaller ones for our cats." KAREN.K

"My Christmas rituals are a mixture of my childhood and then my own children's. My wife Vicki would make up the stockings and I would fill the pillowcases. The stockings for my children were hung off the end of the bed by the pillow cases. My wife worked late into the night while I drowsed. I was a fairly useless husband, slightly better as a father, I hope." PETER.P

"One visiting adult of 50 years old had to have his stocking! We put a *Toblerone* and an orange in an airline support stocking for him." JAN.S

"My Mum usually gives my brother and I a stocking each filled with small gifts and it is usually sat next to the fireplace each year. However little Joshua, my first nephew, arrived three months ago and there seems to be no stockings anymore for Craig and I, but two for Joshua! We've been demoted!" CHARLOTTE.H

"We all get new socks in our Christmas stockings along with useful things like bubble bath and toothbrushes. There are always chocolate coins, some other form of chocolate and a clementine at the bottom, usually found rotting under the kids beds a couple of weeks later."
BRONIA.S

"In my stocking I just get sweets and a satsuma because my Mum likes to put in what she had when she was little."
ANNABEL, AGE.9

SUPER-SIZE
The largest Christmas stocking in Britain was made in 2007 by volunteers who knitted squares for *The Children's Society*. 33m long, 15m wide, it weighed the same as five reindeer.

"Dad's long woolly shooting socks stand in as stockings and are left outside my bedroom door for Christmas morning, there is always a *Terry's Chocolate Orange* and a clementine!" LAURA.M

"When we were much younger (1940s!) we had pillowcases on the end of the bed. As money was not plentiful we always looked for an orange, some chocolate half-crowns and a small gift or two. Oh! and usually a Christmas hat and cracker which were used for the Christmas Day lunch!" JOY.B

"Always a stocking at end of bed and FC tiptoes in and fills with small toys, chocs, tangerine, soap, paper and pens for thank-you letters." REBECCA.S

"We have never had stockings in our house." RACHAEL H

"Stockings, yes. They were hung up by the fireplace and appeared on our bed in the morning - we could open them (i.e. don't wake the parents!) and it would end up that we all went into one bed (siblings only) and opened together. We would then walk about upstairs with big stage whispers until parents got up – we were not allowed downstairs under any circumstances. I still love stockings now!" SARA.F

"Our young people hung up pillowcases on their bedroom door handles. I say young, but youngest is 17 and oldest 23!" STEVE.Y

"We always have *Terry's Chocolate Oranges* in our stockings but one year, Mum didn't get one. I don't know why. It was a mystery." FIONA, AGE.10

"Some walking socks of my husband hung up for the children (well dangled on the fireplace so we didn't spoil the decorations)." GEMMA.L

"Jonathan puts his on the door handle, mine goes at the end of the bed. Both were homemade from our parents that we used growing up." LISA.C

"When the children were little at end of their beds, they say they still hear his bell in the night!" TRACY.G

"My sister and I had stockings our mother had made us when we were born. They are felt, each with a different depiction of Christmas on them and decorated with sequins. In the morning they'd be loaded with sweets and small gifts." BRETT.C

"My wife had made some beautiful hand embroidered stockings which three years ago (and it still upsets) were lost in a property move. She replaced with some fancy ones from America which are really pretty, but so narrow they are hard to put things in!" MARTIN.K

"We always use football socks which stretch out to over a metre. High-status presents are wrapped, silly/low-status ones are not. It's very important that the final stockings are all different shapes, bulgy is good!" JUDITH.Y

"In the 60s, large knitted Stockings by my Mother for each child. Christa had a Father Christmas on red background, Robin had a Christmas tree on white. Hung at the end of the bed by their Father dressed up in his PhD gown (it WAS red after all) whilst they were nearly asleep. Sadly no Father Christmas now." JUNE.B

"The stockings cost an arm and a leg but they come out every year so they're worth it." LESLEY.J

THE BREAKFAST

Everyone starts with Baileys,
even the dog…

THE BREAKFAST

"Everyone starts with Baileys,
even the dog. Oh yes, he loves
a bit of alcohol at this time of
year." replied *Hollie-Rose.C* when
I asked her to tell me about her
Christmas Day. Like so many people
I interviewed, *Hollie-Rose* initially said
her family didn't have any unique
Christmas traditions.

THE BREAKFAST

"We had to sing a carol at M and D's bedroom door, usually *Away in a Manger* at 7am. Then someone would get trays and tea/coffee. We'd all (x3 kids) pile into/ onto their bed and all open stockings together. Then breakfast." REBECCA.S

"We never eat breakfast (unless you count a half tub of Celebrations as breakfast)." NATASHA.M

"We start with a glass of champagne. Later we have smoked salmon, scrambled eggs, grilled bacon, sausages tomatoes and toast." AUDREY.H

"We have the first crackers with breakfast, then it's more crackers every time we eat – really it's crackers all day long." MELANIE.F

"We always have tinned sausages and beans on toast, and Bucks Fizz." ANDREW.B

"We start with chocolate from the stockings as it's a real treat to have chocolate in our house before lunch! Often a glass of sparkling about 11." SALLY.W

"Neil does pancakes for breakfast for everyone." LESLEY.J

"We start with a rum and Coke (having already gone through the small presents altogether as Jess wakes up fiendishly early)." JOE.H

"As adults we start Christmas day with a huge jug of Bloody Marys then start opening presents – still in pyjamas of course. It's become a rule that you can't in fact get dressed until you've opened all your presents (as a child this naturally happened but as an adult someone would often attempt to go up and get dressed and be shouted down by the rest of us)." SARA.F

"Croissants, homemade Stollen, Bucks Fizz and charcuterie for breakfast." STEPHANIE.A

"We start with a cup of tea and biscuits" LEIGH.A

"We pop the bubbly as early as possible in our house and have a glass with breakfast." NATASHA.W

"As a child, breakfast was chocolate bars from selection boxes." EMMA.R

"We start with Buck's Fizz and a proper breakfast at the table, including tea, real coffee and toast. We then may have sherry and mince pies or shortbread while the Christmas phone calls are made and the neighbours' cards are delivered. There's plenty of people in the street all wishing each other Merry Christmas." ANNE.P

"Smoked salmon and cream cheese blinis with a Bucks Fizz or two." CHILLY.H

"We have a late breakfast and look out for our Christmas Robin to come into the garden. We all chill and pretend we don't care, then get excited when he arrives." JESS.H

"Breakfast is banned in our house so as to keep everyone hungry enough for the lunch food!" SAMIRA.S

"Wherever we are in the world at Christmas (up a mountain, a volcano, or in the desert) I have to carry a chilled jar of caviar, chopped egg, chopped onion and Melba toast for breakfast. It can be a challenge." JILL.G

"My Mum always makes Nigella's Christmas Morning Muffins – they're delicious with butter and marmalade. She even made them in Hong Kong." SHEFFIELD.F.M

"My Dad's family had pork pie for Christmas breakfast and Mum's had eggs and ham. When they got married neither would compromise so they had all three, and that's what we've had for the last 61 years." KEITH.F

"Hannah and I go to my parents for breakfast followed by a walk for just my Mum and I." DOM.D.V

"On Xmas morning we get a bit bored after breakfast as we're not allowed to open our presents until everyone is awake, and my Auntie Nell takes ages to wake up." MARIAH, AGE.7

OPENING PRESENTS

*We always have bacon sandwiches and
a cup of tea first...*

OPENING PRESENTS

When I told Bob, my brother-in-law, that *The Normal British Christmas?* was inspired by the Morris family and their frustrating custom of opening the presents in the afternoon he replied, "That's good then, because we do it the proper way."

OPENING PRESENTS

"We are all allowed one present on Christmas Eve, has to be from a C or a D class relative, never an A class relative." RICH.S

"On Christmas Eve kids can open a very small present, they can choose it out of a selection." COLLETTE.B

"Me and Mark opened our presents on Christmas Eve, we couldn't wait and we always do this." JASMINA.J

"One present on Christmas Eve – you could choose it unless the donor of the gift asked you to wait till Christmas day then you'd have to chose something else." SARA.F

"Midnight Mass, then open some presents." MOLLIE.K

"Christmas Day. Presents Opened? The minute the kids woke us." YASMIN.W

"Open presents? Whenever kids drag me out of bed – last year 4am." SAMANTHA.D

"Well before breakfast, more like daybreak!!! No ceremony just joy. Manic." JUNE.B

"First thing in the morning – I think the children would burst if we made them wait." GEMMA.L

"As children, as soon as we woke up and it was the biggest boxes first and it was a crazy frenzy until they were all done." MICHAEL.K

"Presents must be opened as soon as you get up! Keeping them until after lunch is torture." RICHARD.U

"One year I changed the clock so Jessica stayed in bed a bit longer. It worked that year, Nigel warned her the next year though!" SALLY.W

"We always opened as soon as we woke up on Christmas

Day. I don't remember any special order only mass chaos and havoc." AMY.H

"When we get up we light candles in the lounge and play Carols – it's a nice and calm start to the present opening." PAUL.S

"First thing, I open presents from Mum and Dad on my own as they are left outside my room." LAURA.M

"As soon as everyone's up and about really. The kids sort of go at it (after being told which one they must save until last), whilst the adults are more reserved and take their time, being as we rarely manage to receive more than about three each!" NATASHA.M

"Before breakfast, but the dogs unwrap theirs first and that is hilarious to watch, should be on *YouTube*." PETE.B

"Obviously before breakfast, we try to hand them out one by one but it doesn't always work that way. I am waiting for my son to be interested in handing them out as it has always been done by the children in both our families." HANNAH.M

"At 8am Jack and his girlfriend Skype each other on Christmas Day to open their presents from each other (he stays at home with his family and she goes to her Grans in Devon). In his girlfriend's family they have CLUES to find their presents, so Jack gets a clue and then goes around the house with his iPad trying to find his present." TINA.K

"Stockings first, then we had to wait for the other presents until Dad had fed all the animals, 8-900 sheep, 100 cows and 3 dogs. Mind you he'd be back by 8.30am but it still felt like ages to wait." CAROLINE.M

"After breakfast. Everyone gets one and opens together, then next round etc. Winner was Phil this year courtesy of his wife who spoiled him. He was still going way after everyone else." JAN.S

CRACKING JOKES
In 1847, the first cracker was invented by London confectioner Tom Smith, based on a sweet wrapper. Today 300 million crackers are pulled in Britain each year – that's a lot of jokes.

"We open them after breakfast, all together in unwrapping mania!" STEPHANIE.A

"In the morning we all get together in the lounge and take it in turns with Christmas music in the background. It is all quite civilised." CHILLY.H

"Often it's a frenzy after breakfast – that's Paul's family's way." EMILY.A

"We always have bacon sandwiches and a cup of tea then open all the presents in no particular order." PATRICK.M

"Sometime after breakfast, because Keith goes to his Mum's first. I have to patrol up and down as Laclan & Ishbel keep making forays to try and reach the presents before he gets back." KAREN.F

"Mid morning. Each person has a pile, bigger is better and the challenge is you have to open the smallest present first and then in order up to the biggest ones. It can take a while." MELANIE.F

"Just before lunch. We all come together as a family (17 this year) and open the presents. We start by one person opening a present and then move onto the next person, but it soon becomes the mania version!" TRACY.H

"After lunch. We move the sofas around the tree, everyone gets a drink, I sit on the floor and act as Elf."
JESS.H

"Presents after lunch – Keen on them waiting – Ritual – Round in a circle – Each present applauded." HENRY.P

"After lunch. Youngest gives them out and then we take it in turn to open one each going round to see what everyone has." LISA.C

"Always mid-afternoon. Nobody is in charge but we all make sure that each of us has a present to open at about the same time. We usually dress up a bit smart, play Christmas music and really LOVE this special part of the day." AUDREY.H

"After the Christmas film, after Granny comes for lunch, then we open our presents" JORDAN, AGE.6

"Late in the afternoon, between main course and dessert. My younger daughter handed them all out and then we opened them." CHRISTOPHER.J

"Before dinner. We always go to my husband's ex. (Sounds weird but true) and about 3pm we all gather in the front room. We've brought all our gifts with us and put them under the tree. We sort them so everybody's got an individual pile and a drink of course, and then unwrap together. It's always fun." ANNE.P

"Just before the Queen's speech we sort the presents and then we open them afterwards." PETER.H

"The family waits for presents until after the Queen. Kids would keep on asking if they could have a present so we'd allow them a small one from under the tree." DAVID.H

"Around 6pm. Opened one at a time, all sat together." ANDY.D

"In the evening after dinner in my parents' living room in front of a log fire listening to Christmas Carols (*Nat King Cole*, *Mario Lanza*, *Johnny Mathis*). We distribute the presents then, when everyone has been given theirs, we open them one by one." NADINE.A

"Mid evening, after Christmas Carols, presents." ALLY.T

"In the evening 18 of us divided up all the presents into piles. A pile for Tia, a pile for Kieran, a pile for me, etc. We then started from the youngest child who opened one present at a time, thanking the person it was from whilst we all watched in anticipation. Five hours later it was my turn (being the oldest)!" MICHELLE.T

"Ever since I was a child I have only opened one of my presents on Christmas day. I like to save them and unwrap one each day until they run out, one year I unwrapped the last one mid January." OLLIE.H

"Son always took his time and played with each toy before he opened another. Daughter always opened everything first. Husband always guessed what he had before he opened them. I just opened and said thank you." DIANE.G

CHRISTMAS DINNER

The goose is on the washing line...

CHRISTMAS DINNER

Is it turkey, goose, capon, duck, salmon, ham, lamb, macaroni cheese, nut roast or Beef Wellington for you? Lots of variety in the delicious *Normal British Christmas* dinners. Lots of mentions of mountains of food too and proclamations of never eating ever again. Followed, after a short interlude, by the arrival of the trifle and seconds all round.

CHRISTMAS DINNER

"Dad gets up at 4am to put the turkey on." NATHAN.A

"When we arrived my son-in-law informed me he had lunch sorted. "The veg is all prepared and the goose is hanging on the washing line." It was! I blame Nigella." JOAN.D

"Turkey and all the trimmings! It's a joint effort as my sister and her husband do the ham and my Dad does the starter and the gravy. This year our turkey was named Trevor and came from a local farm just a few miles away." LAURA.M

"Turkey (dare I say it always cooked best at my house, needless to say we were somewhere else this year), I was outvoted on trying goose." GEMMA.L

"It was always turkey, if the cat didn't get it – he succeeded twice. One year my Mum went into the kitchen to see the cat astride the turkey with all four claws dug in. The turkey was served carved that year."
PETER.B

"It's a frantic rush to get the meal ready on time, my Dad (a former chef) cooks and my Mum tidies up. By 11.30am it's all in, my Dad has a beer in his hand and my Mum has her PR face on ready to greet everybody. Then we eat more than anyone has ever eaten before." RICH.S

"We always ate in time to all sit down and watch the Queen's speech and it was no starter but a mountain of turkey, stuffing, three or four veg and of course both roast and mash potatoes." MICHAEL.K

"Tips for the perfect Turkey? We always follow the Waitrose instructions." SAMANTHA.D

"We have turkey and trimmings as well as sweet potato and rice and peas. Then Christmas Cake and Jamaican Cake – what's the difference? Rum. The latter is made by my Mum who is teetotal, it's lethal." CAROLYN.W

"We serve dinner for fifty people on Christmas Day. We have two giant turkeys cooked in the church hall kitchen (as well as an extra just-in-case one I cooked in the Vicarage) but I tell my family – nobody's having any turkey until we make sure everyone else has some!"
ANDREA.F.M

"We had turkey this year, but we've been trying to have a range of interesting roasts over the last few years – three bird roast, goose, and so on. We had considered having grouse or pheasant this year, but it started seeming a high risk thing to be experimenting with cooking for the first time on Christmas Day." CHRISTOPHER.J

"We usually go traditional, but had lamb last year. We were in Wales!" EMILY.A

"For 30 years we have had a special nut roast with a red wine gravy as the main dish for Christmas dinner. Our youngest Caolan (who is a big meat eater) complained that he was 'deprived'. When I asked on what planet, he said he asked, and every child in his school had turkey for Christmas dinner and he was the only one that didn't. He now has a turkey steak. He's over the moon." BRONIA.S

"Christmas Day standing rib roast, roast root veg, fancy Brussels, horseradish, gorgeous gravy, set fire to the Christmas pudding." NANCY.W

"I help Granny cook the dinner, we always have the same thing – turkey, macaroni pie and dumplings. The macaroni pie is my favourite." KYLIE, AGE.8

"Beef Wellington with all the trimmings." STEPHANIE.A

"As a child, Christmas dinner was always a capon, roast and three veg very simple, very Methodist. As an adult, I was amazed by all these things people need for Christmas dinner. Brandy Butter? Bread sauce?" JOHNNY.M

"Big fat goose." PETER.P

"Dinner consists of roast beef which is washed down with champagne! (My Grandad & I are not fans of turkey so my Nan sacrifices the normal Christmas turkey element). Then after recovery from the massive plate of food, it's time for pudding. The male figures of the family have spotted dick and custard and the female members have gateaux." SAM.S

"I always cook a large macaroni cheese for everyone." CASSIE R

"To wash everything down we had an abundance of fizzy drinks and juices, mango, orange, grape juices and my favourite – cream soda." GRACE.F

"Roast chicken (they hate turkey so I went with it), roast potatoes / parsnips / carrots, steamed broccoli and sprouts, pigs in blankets, stuffing balls." PETER.H

"This year soup, fish course (lobster, prawns, crab, salmon), turkey, trifle, cheese." MARTIN.K

"We had a four bird roast joint (turkey, chicken, duck, goose) with all the traditional veg and trimmings." JEFF.A

"Everything! Turkey, ham, goose, potatoes, Brussels sprouts, cumin carrots, roast potato, turnip and mash, red cabbage and raisins, trifle and cheese for pudding." DEBRA.W

"My husband cooks the dinner, I do the table decorations and the starters, we always have to have prawns in some form or other for starters, this year it's Prawn Coronets." LEIGH.A

"In my family there's always a rivalry (between the siblings) as to who can sit down to Christmas dinner first, 1.45pm is the latest anyone has sat down ever!" JANE.B

"We put all the Yorkshire puddings in a bowl and half way through the children can have one each. Then one more at the end." JANE.H

"The dog and cats had turkey with a little gravy." KAREN.K

"My Mum has become a vegetarian, but still makes the beef gravy for me." HOLLIE-ROSE.C

"We always do Christmas lunch at 2pm – my brother lives in Norway now and we FaceTime each other's food." KRAY, AGE.8

"All have to wear our Christmas hats throughout the lunch, spares if yours fall off." DOM.D.V

"Our Dad worked as a postman and had to work on Christmas Morning. He was very popular and everyone would ask him to join them in a toast. Lunch was always delayed while he slept it off." JIM.M

"We do have crackers, but my Dad won't have one or pull one." EMMA.R

"One year my mother-in-law's dog knocked the flaming pudding out from her hands. She screamed then myself and others scooped it off the floor and we all ate it. Such wonderful memories" MARGARET.H

"LOTS of chocolate. Spiced apple and rum hot toddies. Homemade pecan pie and cinnamon ice cream for dessert." STEPHANIE.A

"Lunch is followed by Christmas pudding, and something else for the awkward ones." HANNAH.M

"Syrup sponge pudding, cheese and biscuits." STEVE.Y

"Personally I don't eat Christmas pudding but I do like a cheesecake!" RACHAEL.H

"Trevor's Mum does a lovely Christmas pudding."
KATHYRN.J

"Then we move onto the desserts, Xmas pud and brandy, trifle and something chocolately for the youth. Then cheese. Then tea and coffee. Then brandy. My sister has a *Baileys*. I'm so claustrophobic by now that even though I can't move, I'm delighted to go on the walk." RICH S

"The pudding was a disaster as overdid it in the microwave. Had a re-run three days later to make up for it." JAN.S

"Always have soup, then a fish course, then turkey which my Dad cooks (and that's unusual). We have loads of Brussels as I love them – then pudding – then a lie down." JILL.S

"I dislike Christmas food (pudding, cake, sprouts, pigs in blankets) so would happily do without it all." GWEN.R

"Buck's Fizz, Salmon, Lamb, Duck, Turkey, Rice & Peas, Roast Potatoes, Brussels Sprouts, Sausages Wrapped in Bacon, Stuffing, Chocolate Log, Christmas Pudding, Brandy & Champagne Cream and Courvoisier Cream, etc. Luckily I was staying at my Mum's so I didn't need to be rolled home!" NADINE.A

"We buy a chocolate cake but everyone too full and so we say we're going to eat it later, but we're all still full – so I wake up in the night and eat it about 3am." JOE.H

"We have a huge plate which is always used for the turkey, it was my husband's grandmother's. Only time it is used." PAM.T

"We always use the special china we were given as a wedding present for Christmas dinner with crystal glasses and we have beautiful little chrome ducks that Marie and Becky bought us one year and they make little place cards to go in them. We have a special set of Christmas napkins too." BRONIA.S

"We always have a paper tablecloth and play maths and logic puzzles on it in between courses." OLLIE.H

"My Mum was a vegetarian for 28 years. It was tasting turkey just after Christmas one year that finally sent her back to the dark side." BEN.M

"One Christmas tradition is to always forget one ingredient in the Christmas dinner – don't do it on purpose but so far it's happened every year! Of course not always the same one – I always remember what I forgot last year and get that!" SIMON.G

"We do have a tradition of trying to fit a tiny piece of every element of the Christmas meal onto one fork and eating that in one huge mouthful. Quite a challenge, given all the trimmings." FRANCO.C

"We go to the pub." CHARLOTTE.K

BRUSSELS SPROUTS

There's always a race...

BRUSSELS SPROUTS

This tiny green vegetable certainly generates strong opinions – *Loathe them* just edging ahead of *Love them* in my research (I'm a *Loather* myself). Clearly though, they are an integral part of the *Normal British Christmas* and, as one British supermarket sells 140 million Brussels sprouts in the two weeks before Christmas, some of you must be eating them.

BRUSSEL SPROUTS

"We now have the Annual Brussels Sprout Competition (having seen it in *The Vicar of Dibley*), Jess is always determined to beat Nigel and they both eat loads. Jess wins." SALLY.W

"I always take some, even though I don't eat them, a fact which I've never questioned before now." EVAN.P

"We always get the lads together on Christmas Eve and the Christmas jumpers come out and there's always a race. 15 of us with wind-up Brussels sprouts. It's hilarious." JOE.H

"I never eat the Brussels on Christmas Day because then they'll be more left over for Boxing Day and fried-up Brussels are delicious!" PETER.B

"I make everyone their own favourites for Christmas lunch – salmon or chicken or steak. Definitely no Brussels for anyone!" LESLEY.J

"This year, I was doing the cooking. Nobody got food poisoning, hurray! They even ate the Brussels!" TASNEEM.K

"I eat one sprout, because it's Christmas." YASMEEN.M

"Mum did amazing stuffings and made awesome sprouts with bacon and chestnuts." REBECCA.S

"Brussels. I don't like the smell. I don't eat them." JOE.H

❄

THE SCIENCE
Did you know that 70% of us carry a gene that makes the brain detect sharp, bitter flavours, resulting in the dislike of Brussels sprouts.

THE AFTERNOON

*The Queen, Julie Andrews
and playing Monopoly ...*

THE AFTERNOON

Do you spend the entire
Christmas day indoors? Or does
your *Normal British Christmas*
include a visit to the park? *Peter.B*
told me about venturing outside
in the afternoon one year, thinking
he might be the only person in the
world not at home.
He wasn't.

THE AFTERNOON

"After lunch we all go in the front room, turn off all the lights and light the candles on the Christmas cake and the alcohol on the Christmas pudding (my Mum makes the cake, we buy the pudding). We all make wishes. Then we light the candles everywhere around the room, then my brother is Santa and my sister and I are elves and we give the presents out." BETHANY, AGE.9

"Brisk walk with the dog wearing Christmas hats. I'm always the last man standing with the Christmas hat."
RICH.S

"If not enough people want to play *Monopoly* in the afternoon then my Mum and I each play two pieces, she's always The Queen and I'm Julie Andrews." RHEA, AGE.9

"My son arrives with a suitcase full of board games." DIANE.E.G

"We always watch *Oliver Twist* and then *Monopoly* comes out and the arguments start. Always the same and all moan but we all love it really." COLLETTE.B

"A post-lunch walk along Southsea seafront, Freddie with his new Scooter. A walk I never do after any other meal during the year!" KEVIN.S

"Always watch *White Christmas*." GILLIAN.B

"In Trivial Pursuit my Dad would join in but would only be 'Phone-A-Friend' although sometimes he couldn't resist it and would shout out the answer. He'd also make up limericks after lunch and pretend to fall over!" LEIGH .A

"Always watch *Muppets Christmas Carol*." PIPPA B

"We play Trivial Pursuit, often myself and my brother against my Dad who has won every year. Until last year." ADAM.L

"After lunch for 50 in the church hall Pete (the Vicar) announced "We'll all watch the Queen's Speech, then have a cup of tea before we go home." Sadly, the Wi-Fi failed so Pete missed it for first time ever." ANDREA.F.M

"My sister, Mum and I always do a bit of 'washing up' to very loud music and dance around the kitchen. My Dad loved doing this when he was alive, so this is something that makes us feel very close to him."
SALLY-ANNE.E

"We watch *The Sound of Music* or *Mary Poppins*. We do like a bit of Julie Andrews at Christmas!" SHELLI.R

"Once Christmas lunch has worn off (it does not!) we have a traditional Christmas tea quite late with everything from fish, shell fish and hams/turkey to salad (homemade pickled onions and beetroot) and cheeses and crackers plus Christmas cake." CHILLY.H

THE QUEEN'S SPEECH
The tradition of the royal Christmas broadcast began in 1932. King George V read a speech by Rudyard Kipling, it began, "I speak now from my home and from my heart, to you all..."

143

"For tea we always have cold turkey, ham, pickles and 'Cheeses for Jesus'. I don't know why it's called that it just always has been. Now my son has Christmas in Australia and his Mother-in-Law does 'Cheeses for Jesus'." JANE.B

"We listen to an old record each year that I love (always the same one), play games in the evening, followed by chocolate log and Christmas cake." LISA.C

"20 of us play *Are you there Moriarty?* Taking turns to try to hit each other with a newspaper'stick'. Rolling out of the way was particuarly important the year my older brother put an actual stick inside the newspaper!" OLLIE.H

"As always, my Mum Vanna, makes her fantastic Christmas cakes for everybody. My husband John makes our wonderful Christmas puddings." DAWN.L

"Charades and chocolates. Brandy. More charades and more chocolate. More brandy. Bed." BOB.C

"We forgot to eat the Christmas cake! It's still in the cupboard." NIKA.G

CLOTHING

A polar bear onesie and a Christmas pudding hat...

CLOTHING

Often, the person you least
expect will surprise you with their
Normal British Christmas outfit.
An elegant Armani-clad friend of
mine confessed she always wears
jazzy Christmas knickers during
December.

CHRISTMAS CLOTHING

"When I first met Jamie his favourite piece of clothing was a pair of red trousers, I had no idea they would come out every Christmas for the next seventeen years." FLICK.B

"I have my Christmas jumper (it turns me into a pudding) and a Christmas tree hat with baubles that light up." TASNEEM.K

"My wife always has Christmas socks and wears reindeer earrings with reindeer antlers on her head – don't ask!" MARTIN.K

"All the men wear a big (homemade) bow tie." FRANCO.C

"Polar bear onsie, polar bear slippers and snowflake jumper." STEPHANIE.A

"We both have Christmas jumpers but as my one has the slogan 'nice baubles' there are only a few occasions/ places I can wear it!" TRACY.H

"I wore a tasteful Christmas jumper. My sister Mona and her family went all out and wore elf outfits." ROSE.Y

"Clarice has a Christmas T-shirt." AMANDA.H

"Santa hats are worn and I wear light-up earrings!" MANDY.R

"Ben has a selection of Christmas ties." JOAN.D

"I love to wear sparkly things at Christmas, the more sequins the better." CHARLOTTE.H

"All men and children had jumpers, men had elf hats too, I had Santa slippers." DIANE.G

"Christmas leggings, pants and socks." SALLY.W

"This year we managed to get my Dad in a Christmas jumper, so we all matched on Christmas day." TONI.J

"My youngest and I had Christmas jumpers, plus we all wore Christmas socks. My Uncle had a sporting Christmas waistcoat which was red, glittery and had 'Ho, Ho, Ho' printed on the back!" PAM.T

"We used to dress up for Christmas lunch but this year we wore our new onesies! Very comfortable and allowed for my expanding waistline!" LAURA.B

"Scarily this year we all opened presents in Onesies (a change from dressing gowns). My mother-in-law wore an army camouflage onesie." GEMMA.L

"My one-year old niece 'chose' to dress up as a Christmas pudding, at least my sister told us it was her choice." TINA.T

"Everyone tends to wear red, especially red onesies."
STEPHANIE E

"I have a rather silly tradition on Christmas Day which is to wear some kind of festive false lashes. I enjoy getting dressed for Christmas lunch and make quite an effort for what is, for some, a day to slob around in PJs!" NATALIE.J

"A silk pair of pyjamas and a cashmere jumper. By wearing a nice pair of pyjamas I don't feel so bad about staying in them all day!" NATASHA.W

"I have a Christmas pudding hat, that I can only wear if my son isn't with me, otherwise he would die of embarassment." TINA.D

"I bought myself a Christmas jumper, not with a crazy picture, just a burnt orange classic Arran style one." MICHELLE.T

"We all have Christmas jumpers, the madder the better, for wearing Christmas Day." PATRICK.M

"I have resolved that next year I MUST have a Christmas jumper." PETER.H

BOXING DAY

Elf hunts and five gold rings ...

BOXING DAY

Is your day action packed – the sales, the walk, football, horse racing? Or is a home day – board games and charades fuelled by leftover sandwiches? I smiled when *Mark.M* told me they always go to a restaurant for Christmas dinner but buy and cook a turkey so they can have 'leftovers' on Boxing Day.

BOXING DAY

"We go outside for 'The Race'. My Uncle evaluates each of us and places us for the start, we have to run up the hill and back to the house (probably about 150m). When we were kids the parents were at the back and we got the head start, now they are all at the front. It takes about 15 minutes to line everyone up, lots of negotiations and distraction, suddenly Uncle shouts "Go" and several miss the start as chatting. No one EVER remembers who won 'The Race' the previous year." REBECCA.S

"Boxing Day – pure laziness, football and films." JOE.H

"We always have a jigsaw on the go and at some point someone usually spills wine on it and we have to wait while pieces dry out on the radiator." CAROLYN.W

"We head to the Sales. We leave early, shops are really packed, sometimes the queue to pay is about an hour." FREIDA.M

"Always at my Mum's for Boxing Day." LEIGH.A

"The Elf Hunt is a must. Everyone has an Elf Hat and everyone has to hide in the house, but has to look for other people too. If you find someone you take their hat. The one with the most hats at the end wins." JEREMY.A

"Always a walk. No option." RUTH.P

"Boxing Day was a complete repeat of the Christmas food. Always my uncles would go to the working men's club together as the women prepared lunch. They always had pints of beer and always there were arguments about politics over the meal. As children we ate at a separate table together and listened to the arguments and conversations of the adults." MICHAEL.K

A PRESENT A DAY
In the song, *The 12 Days of Christmas*, there are 364 gifts altogether, so one for each day of the year except Christmas Eve.

154

"On Boxing Day my Grandaughter and I make gingerbread men for the family for tea." LESLEY.J

"Boxing Day memories? Uncle Harry arriving, presents shown, presents played with, films watched." JOHNNY.M

"We get together with all the cousins and families on Boxing Day, we were x14, but now with next generation can be as many as x31. We go to my aunt's who has space and at lunch we always sing *The 12 days of Christmas* in groups of two or three for each day. You have to stand up every time it comes to you, we're all terrible singers but it's always funny. One cousin can sing, so she always gets *Five Gold Rings*!" REBECCA.S

"When we are at home we always cook more veg on Christmas Day so that we can have bubble and squeak on Boxing Day." PAM.T

"Boxing Day? *Cluedo* will always be a part of it." JESS.H

"Boxing day there may be cold meats, salad and gherkins. I love gherkins, (so much so that I had them in my stocking one year)." ANNE.P

"Lunch is a soup made from stock from the carcass."
PETER.H

"My cousin only comes around once a year, on Boxing Day, so I get very happy on Boxing Day." FREDRIC, AGE.6

"We tend to swap round from house to house in-laws, parents, siblings. Usually lots of Kir Royale to drink and some charades played, with much hilarity." GEMMA.L

WHY WE LOVE CHRISTMAS

The best bit is when my Dad puts the mistletoe behind his ears...

WHY WE LOVE CHRISTMAS

"Family and friends." Everybody
said it. *"Looking forward to being
with family and friends."* *"Enjoying
being with family and friends."*
*"Remembering being with family
and friends."* It was the
great agreement.

WHY WE LOVE CHRISTMAS

"I can't remember any presents I got as a child, just lots and lots of happiness." PETER.B

"The best bit? Christmas morning, before the presents, when everyone is so excited." CAROLYN.W

"Children being friends ALL day." CHARLOTTE.K

"Sometimes I take my family for granted and I don't go to visit as much as I should and when we're all crammed into one house together it makes me wonder why I don't. I love these weirdos." BRETT.C

"For us in our 'latter' years it is great to have the family together, even for so short a time, it is a time to treasure." JOY.B

"My Mum. One Christmas she stayed up all night to make me a huge Spitfire aeroplane out of Meccano, a very tired and sore fingered mum in the morning... and a huge grin on my face." ROBIN.P

"A special Christmas memory would be my boyfriend proposing at the side of a mountain in Val d'Isere. I said yes." CHARLOTTE.H

"Best thing? We go to Ghana and miss it all!" TONY.F

"The best thing is the way the world goes quiet and business stops, family gathers, there's kindness and generosity and awe and a feeling of connection to those who have gone before us and are far away from us as well as those next to us at the table." NANCY.W

"It was always my Mum. As a child, our main present was often something to wear that my Mum had made in secret." CATHERINE.M.S

"Every year, I love the family coming to us, yet very much miss my Dad, so having the opportunity to talk about him with everyone there is fab." SALLY-ANNE.E

"First the thing I don't love, my son is now in Australia and the first few Christmases were utterly heartbreaking. I am so very thankful for my family that are still here." JANE.B

"Family. This year was hard as my eldest son bought a house and so he and his girlfriend only came round to us at tea time - I hated him not being there when we woke up on Christmas morning." PAM.T

"The best thing about Christmas was having my parents and my brother join me at my new house. Last Christmas was my last at home so pretty emotional. It was nice to be with all my favourites and not miss them so much." TASNEEM.K

"The best thing has to be that great gathering on Christmas Day. Every parent, step parent, half brother, step sister and half sister of a step sister, to one event. It's amazing when we're all together, we're so loud." ANNE.P

FESTIVE TRIPS
4.25 million British people travel each abroad year and celebrate their *Normal British Christmas* in another country.

"The best thing about Christmas was introducing my new partner to my family and having him over for Christmas dinner." GRACE.F

"Seeing three brothers who don't usually see each other get together." JAN.S

"Last year we did everything the same as always, just with a baby. Made it even more special." DOM.D.V

"Having the grandchildren around and being the biggest kid in the house!" TRACY.G

"The coolest Christmas ever was when I was 13 and thought I'm not going to stay in this year! I went to the park and was amazed – people were playing football – I joined in. It was the best Christmas EVER." PETER.B

"As a child, getting the BIG PRESENT. One year I got motorised Lego. It was brilliant. Actually it's never been beaten." JOHNNY.M

"I like watching all the happy films at Christmas – makes me feel the world is a better place." NAJIA.K

"I remember, aged about six, reaching into my pillow case and feeling a flat baize surface. I was thrilled at its touch. When dawn came I saw that it was the flat top of a bus conductor's peaked cap. There was the whole uniform. I came down stairs dressed in it and found my grandmother (at whose house we were staying) on her knees with a dustpan and brush cleaning up Santa's sooty footprints and having a good grumble at his carelessness." PETER.P

"Now Trevor can ski, hooray, that's Christmas sorted."
OLGA.K

"At Christmas when my brother and sisters and I get together we always laugh about other Christmas times. Like the year we were all dressed up (Jane, our oldest sister loved to dress up) and just before we left my brother cracked an egg on her head." SALLY.W

"The best bit is when my Dad puts the mistletoe behind his ears, he always does it." SIENNA, AGE.7

"When you have grown up children it's the one time you're all together. I love it!" MAUREEN.B

"We always share a Jamaican drink called Sorrel and Christmas cake which is soaked in rum. The best bit of Christmas is being with family and friends, and Sorrel!" NADINE.A

"I like how it symbolises the end of one year and the beginning of the next. It's a time for renewal and reflection." CHRISTOPHER.J

"My Mum's favourite bit is the Christmas dinner, because we don't have it very often she really enjoys it."
GLORIA, AGE.6

THE LAST WORD

No traditions for us, all just normal...

THE
LAST WORD

I hope you, the reader, have enjoyed this peek into people's lives and homes during the festive period, and that, like me, you have found how other people celebrate their *Normal British Christmas* fascinating. I have both laughed and been extremely moved by what people shared, so massive thanks to everyone quoted for your time and for allowing me to include all the entertaining, amazing, poignant and daft things you do.

I feel sure there's more to discover. If you would like to share your *Normal British Christmas* stories with me please do, I look forward to reading them! **Tee D**
Facebook: *TheNormalBritishChristmas?*
Email: nbc@teedobinson.com

THE LAST WORD

"My boyfriend's family came for Christmas and on the day I panicked. I didn't know what to do in what order, it wasn't 'my Christmas'. It was still fun in the end, just very strange." JESS.S

"I had a lovely trip down memory lane while thinking about your Christmas questions. Thank you!" TERESA.S

"Writing our Christmas answers for you has been great and really cathartic as our guests left this morning and we are all feeling a bit sad. Are you going to do something with the information?" JAN.S

"No traditions for us, all just normal." PATRICK.M

ABOUT THE AUTHOR

Tee Dobinson is a Motivational Speaker, Event MC and Kindness Advocate.
She loves London, tall buildings, people and, obviously, Christmas.

teedobinson.com
🐦 @TeeDobinson
📘 TheNormalBritishChristmas?

Also written/edited by Tee Dobinson
Treasures of the Guildhall Art Gallery
Inside Tower Bridge
The Monument
Tower Bridge 360°
The Gherkin Guide
360° at the Gherkin
The Mummy Glue
The Portrait Perspective
The Swiss Re Cookbook for the NSPCC
The Crunch (with Karen Amen)